Europe

What an exciting continent to learn about!

- Europe is next to the smallest of the seven continents.
- Several island countries are a part of Europe.
- People from dozens of cultures, speaking dozens of languages live on the continent.
- It shares a boundary with Asia. Sometimes the two are considered one continent called Eurasia.
- Even though Europe is a small continent it has a large population.
- Part of Europe is above the Arctic Circle.
- The climate varies from icy cold in the far north to warm sunshine in the Mediterranean.
- Much of the music and art of the Western world has come from Europe.

Find Europe on this map.
Color it and write Europe across the center of the continent.

A Physical Map of Europe

Let's Look Europe

Find these places and mark them on this map of Europe.
Use a map, a globe or an atlas to help you find the answers.

O Black Sea

O Atlantic Ocean

O English Channel

O Baltic Sea

O Gulf of Bothnia

O Mediterranean Sea

O Adriatic Sea

O Bay of Biscay

O Caspian Sea

O Aegean Sea

O Crimea Peninsula

O Central Russian Uplands

O Iberian Peninsula

O Kola Peninsula

O Grampian Mountains

O Swiss Alps

O Carpathian Mountains

O Apennines

O Pyrenees

O Caucasus Mountains

O Volga River

O Seine River

O Danube River

O Rhine River

O Thames River

O Loire River

O Po River

O Vistula River

O Dnieper River

O Guadaqiuvir River

Note: Give your students a copy of the map on page 2 for this activity.

Environments

Although Europe is a small continent, it has many different natural environments. There is frozen tundra in the far north, large mountain ranges throughout the continent a large north-central plain, and warm, sunny countries in the south.

Many parts of Europe are close to water. There are oceans, seas, and gulfs around three sides of Europe. There are long rivers, fjords, and lakes throughout the continent

Many islands surround the main land mass of Europe. Some are very small while others, such as the United Kingdom, form a whole country.

---

1. Color in these areas:
   mountains - dark green
   oceans, rivers, lakes - blue
   Great European Plain - yellow
   islands - brown

2. Name two of the mountain ranges of Europe.

   _____   _____

3. Name two rivers in Europe.

   _____   _____

4. Name two seas that border Europe.

   _____   _____

Bonus: You may need to use an atlas to help you with the bonus tasks.
   • Find a peninsula. Circle it with black.
   • Find a fjord. Circle it with red.
   • Find an area above the Arctic Circle. Color it light blue.

               Europe

A Political Map of Europe

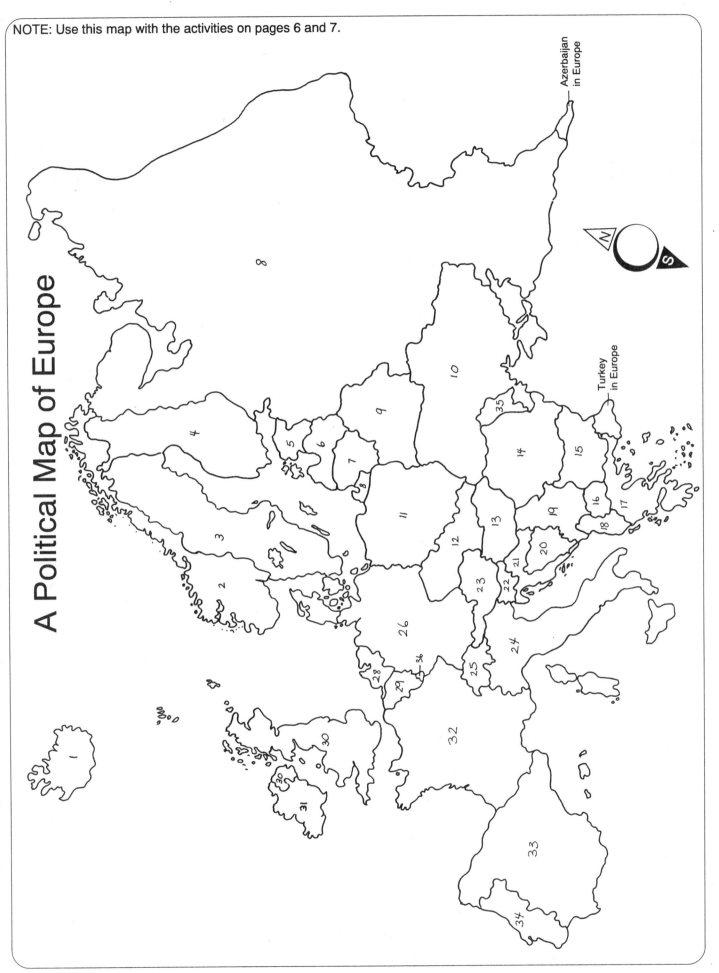

Azerbaijan in Europe

Turkey in Europe

Europe

Note: Give each child a copy of the map on page 5 to use with this activity. Have maps and atlases available. Use the activity for individual or partner work.

The Countries of Europe

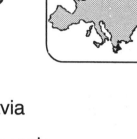

Look at your map.
Find the number for each country.
Write the number on the correct line.

___ Albania	___ Latvia
___ Austria	___ Lithuania
___ Belgium	___ Luxembourg
___ Bosnia and Hercegovina	___ Moldova
___ Bulgaria	___ Netherlands
___ Byelarus	___ Norway
___ Croatia	___ Poland
___ Czechoslovakia	___ Portugal
___ Denmark	___ Romania
___ Estonia	___ Russia
___ Finland	___ Slovenia
___ France	___ Spain
___ Germany	___ Sweden
___ Greece	___ Switzerland
___ Hungary	___ Ukraine
___ Iceland	___ United Kingdom
___ Ireland	___ Yugoslavia
___ Italy	

Bonus:
Some countries are so small they do not show on this map.
Find where they are located and put an X to mark the spot.

1 - Vatican City   **2** - Monaco   **3** - Andorra

4 - Liechtenstein   **5** - Malta   **6** - San Marino

               Europe

Note: Children will need copies of their political maps and/or an atlas for this activity.

North, South, East or West?

Use the compass rose on your map to help you fill in this chart.

To get from...	Go North	Go South	Go East	Go West
Romania to Bulgaria				
Germany to Belguim				
Hungary to Czechoslovakia				
Norway to Denmark				
Sweden to Russia				
Poland to Germany				
France to the United Kingdom				
Macedonia to Yugoslavia				
Switzerland to Italy				
Lithuania to Latvia				
Finland to Estonia				
Byelarus to Ukraine				

Europe

Find the Countries

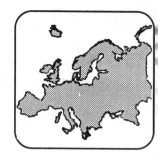

```
U N I T E D K I N G D O M F R A N C E W
B D E N M A R K N B S A U S T R I A U O
E I P I T A L Y O U P R E I N D E E R L
L C O N E T H E R L A N D S Q R S T O V
G E R M A N Y Q W G I W U R A L W N P E
I L T B G O L S A A N O U G R E E C E R
U A U O A R A W Y R A L P S W E D E N I
M N G A R T P I S I P F B H A R E G O N
Q D A R E H P T E A E L E M M I N G F E
P O L A N D C Z E C H O S L O V A K I A
R L I E C H T E N S T E I N N F S S N B
U I R E L A N R R O M A N I A O K T L I
S C E I F F E L T O W E R O C X I O A G
S E A H U N G A R Y C H A M O I S R N B
I V A T I C A N C I T Y F J O R D K D E
A L B A N I A D L U X E M B O U R G Y N
H E D G E H O G G I B R A L T A R O X B
```

Albania	France	Poland
Alps	Germany	Portugal
Austria	Gibraltar	reindeer
Belgium	Greece	Romania
Big Ben	hare	Russia
Bulgaria	hedgehog	sea
chamois	Hungary	Spain
Czechoslovakia	Iceland	stork
Denmark	Italy	Sweden
Eiffel tower	lemming	Switzerland
Europe	Liechtenstein	United Kingdom
fjord	Luxembourg	Vatican City
Finland	Monaco	wolverine
	Netherlands	
	Norway	

Bonus:
Underline the animals you find in the word list.
Put a check mark by every country name in your word list that has three syllables.

         Europe

Note: Provide almanacs, atlases, library books and encyclopedias for children to use to complete this activity. Children may work individually or in pairs to complete the assignment.

The People of Europe

Europe is made up of many small countries. The countries in the far north contain the fewest people, while the central and southern countries have large populations. These populations, especially in the cities, have been increasing with the arrival of immigrants from other continents. There are dozens of different languages spoken across the continent. There are many different cultures and religions among the various people living there.

Some of the countries of Europe are very old and have not changed boundaries in hundreds of years. Others have only recently become independent countries.

Much of the land, especially in the Great European Plain, is used for farming. Cattle, sheep and hogs are also raised. Because so many parts of Europe are near the sea, fishing is an important industry. Mining and manufacturing make many of Europe's cities into important world economic leaders.

Choose five countries in Europe.
Find this information about each country.

Country	*capital city*	*money used*	*main language*	*main products*

 Europe

The Animals of Europe

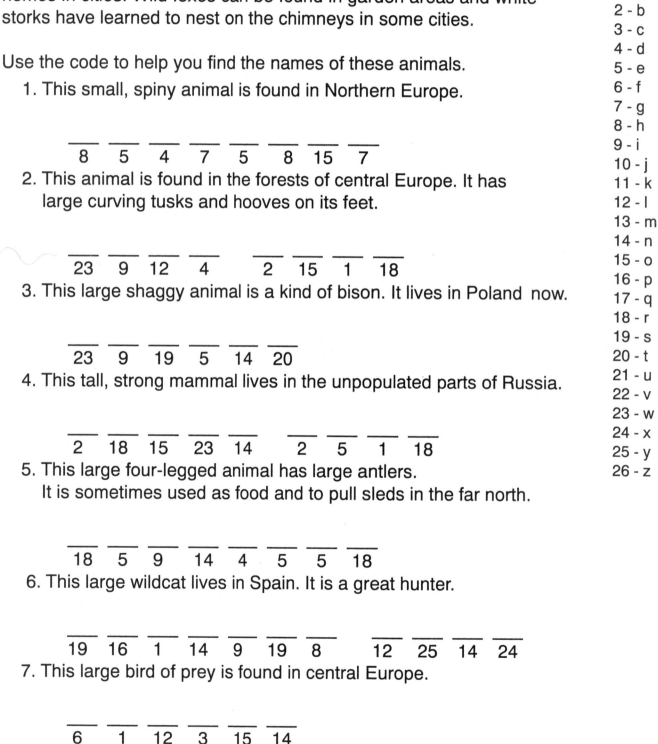

There is not as much open land in Europe as on many of the other continents. Because so many forests and open spaces have been become farms and cities, there is less area for wild animals to live. In the wild areas that do exist and in national parks and game preserves, the animals that once ran wild throughout the continent can still be found. Some wild animals have learned to make their homes in cities. Wild foxes can be found in garden areas and white storks have learned to nest on the chimneys in some cities.

Use the code to help you find the names of these animals.

1. This small, spiny animal is found in Northern Europe.

  __ __ __ __ __ __ __ __
  8 5 4 7 5 8 15 7

2. This animal is found in the forests of central Europe. It has large curving tusks and hooves on its feet.

  __ __ __ __   __ __ __ __
  23 9 12 4   2 15 1 18

3. This large shaggy animal is a kind of bison. It lives in Poland now.

  __ __ __ __ __ __
  23 9 19 5 14 20

4. This tall, strong mammal lives in the unpopulated parts of Russia.

  __ __ __ __ __   __ __ __ __
  2 18 15 23 14   2 5 1 18

5. This large four-legged animal has large antlers. It is sometimes used as food and to pull sleds in the far north.

  __ __ __ __ __ __ __ __
  18 5 9 14 4 5 5 18

6. This large wildcat lives in Spain. It is a great hunter.

  __ __ __ __ __ __ __   __ __ __ __
  19 16 1 14 9 19 8   12 25 14 24

7. This large bird of prey is found in central Europe.

  __ __ __ __ __ __
  6 1 12 3 15 14

Code
1 - a
2 - b
3 - c
4 - d
5 - e
6 - f
7 - g
8 - h
9 - i
10 - j
11 - k
12 - l
13 - m
14 - n
15 - o
16 - p
17 - q
18 - r
19 - s
20 - t
21 - u
22 - v
23 - w
24 - x
25 - y
26 - z

Search Cards

What is the highest point in Europe? How high is it?

What is the name of the mountain range separating Europe and Asia?

What are fjords? Where will you find them?

What is the longest river in Europe?

Where is the only place in Europe where monkeys live in the wild?

What large country in Europe is also a large part of Asia?

Which countries in Europe reach above the Arctic Circle?

Which European countries border the Mediterranean Sea?

Which two countries are separated by the Pyrenees Mountains?

What is the smallest country in size and population in Europe? Where is it located?

What is the name of the island off the tip of Italy?

What are the names of the four countries in the United Kingdom?

What country forms the eastern boundary of Portugal?

What large island belonging to Denmark is considered a part of the North American continent?

Make up a question about Europe. Write it on a card. See if your classmates can answer your question.

Crossword Puzzle

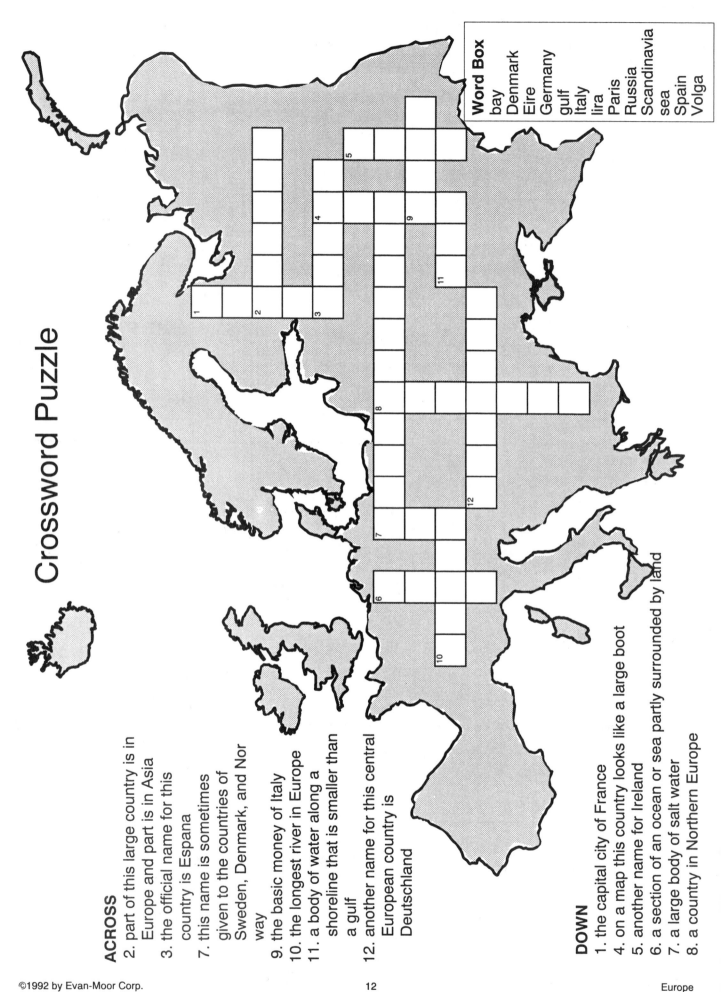

Word Box

bay
Denmark
Eire
Germany
gulf
Italy
lira
Paris
Russia
Scandinavia
sea
Spain
Volga

ACROSS

2. part of this large country is in Europe and part is in Asia
3. the official name for this country is Espana
7. this name is sometimes given to the countries of Sweden, Denmark, and Norway
9. the basic money of Italy
10. the longest river in Europe
11. a body of water along a shoreline that is smaller than a gulf
12. another name for this central European country is Deutschland

DOWN

1. the capital city of France
4. on a map this country looks like a large boot
5. another name for Ireland
6. a section of an ocean or sea partly surrounded by land
7. a large body of salt water
8. a country in Northern Europe

Europe

Name_____ Date_____

Books I've Read
about
Europe

Date	Title	Author		Rating
		Author	☐ fiction	
		Illustrator	☐ picture	
			☐ nonfiction	
		Author	☐ fiction	
		Illustrator	☐ picture	
			☐ nonfiction	
		Author	☐ fiction	
		Illustrator	☐ picture	
			☐ nonfiction	
		Author	☐ fiction	
		Illustrator	☐ picture	
			☐ nonfiction	
		Author	☐ fiction	
		Illustrator	☐ picture	
			☐ nonfiction	
		Author	☐ fiction	
		Illustrator	☐ picture	
			☐ nonfiction	

My **Favorite** Book about Europe

_____

_____

_____

_____

Europe

A Travel Guide to Europe

Involve children in writing about what they have learned about the countries of Europe. The finished results become a class book. Each child will need a copy of the political map on page 5 and the **My Trip to _____** form on page 15. He/She will also need a sheet of drawing paper the same size as the two forms.

Brainstorm

List all of the countries of Europe your class can recall.
Discuss interesting facts about each country.
Have each child select a country for an imaginary trip.

Gather Information

Children will need access to an atlas, encyclopedias, and/or library books on the countries they have chosen. They need to think about and locate information to answer the following questions.

What country are you visiting?
How will you get there (mode of transportation, arrival point)?
Where will you go in the country?
What will you see? do? eat?
Tell interesting facts about points of interest in the country.

Production

1. Fill in **"My Trip to _____"** form.

2. Color in the country you are visiting on your map of Europe. Write in the name of the country and the name of the capital city on your map.

3. Draw a picture showing one or more points of interest in your country to use as a title page for this mini-report.

4. Have each child put his/her three pages together. Assemble the countries in alphabetical order and staple them in a cover to make a class book. Put it in your class library for everyone to share.

Europe

Note: Reproduce this page to use with the writing assignment on page 14.

My Trip to ______________________

Basic Information:

- Capital City ______________
- Population ______________
- Language spoken ______________
- Currency ______________

How I got there:

____

____

____

____

____

____

Three interesting things I did...

____

____

____

____

____

____

____

____

____

____

____

____

____

____

My favorite city was ______________

I liked it because...

____

____

____

____

____

____

Here I am enjoying ______________.

Using Your Posters

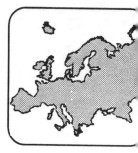

Poster 1 - **Map of Europe**

• Use the map on this poster to help children learn the names of the countries of Europe.

• Use it to practice locating places in relation to the Arctic Circle.

• Use it to practice finding places based on the directions shown on the compass rose.

• Use the poster as part of a bulletin board display to create interest in the continent of Europe.

• Post it in an easily seen area for reference as children do the activities in this unit.

• Put it and an atlas into a center with the Search Cards on page 11.

Poster 2 - **Picture of European Elements**

• Use this poster to encourage children to find information using books, maps and an atlas.

• Use the illustration as a part of a bulletin board display.

• Have children find the location of each plant, animal, person or place shown in the illustration. The names are printed on the poster. Cover these names up if you wish to make the task more difficult for your students.

• Have children work in pairs or small groups to find out more about the items in the illustration. Each groups should pick one element to research. Provide time for students to share what they discover.

• Use the poster to motivate creative writing experiences. Children can select areas of the poster to use as a basis for a story, poem, newspaper article, etc.

 Europe